BACKYARD BIRDS

CARDINALS

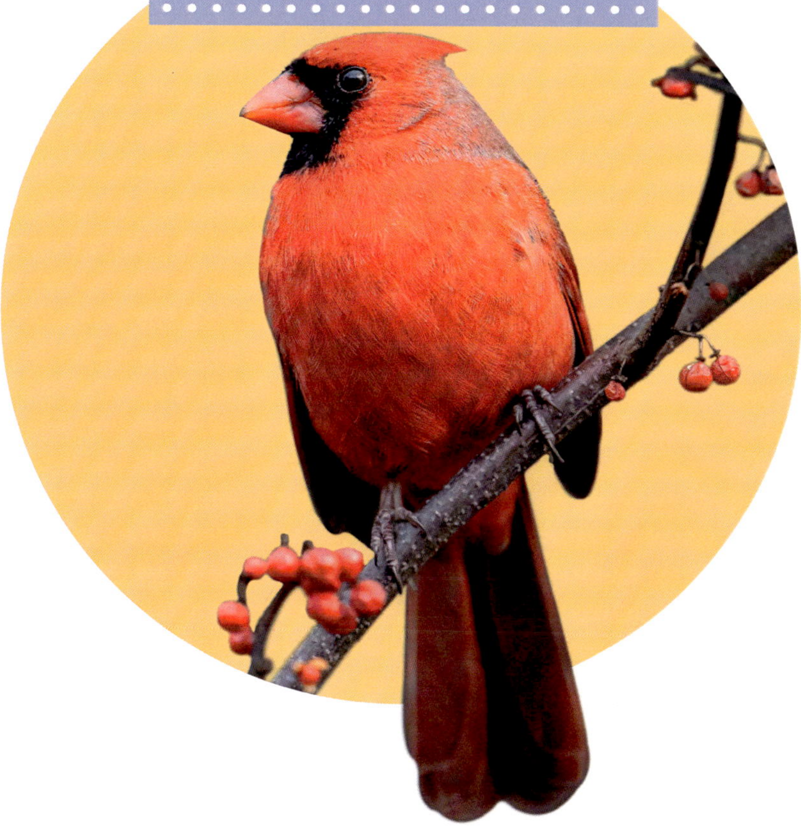

by Anastasia Suen

crest

nest

Look for these words and pictures as you read.

bald

bill

Have you seen this bird?
A cardinal has red feathers.
Males are all red.

crest

Females are red and brown.
Head feathers point up.
They make a crest.

nest

Mom makes a round nest.
It looks like a cup.
The eggs have lots of spots.

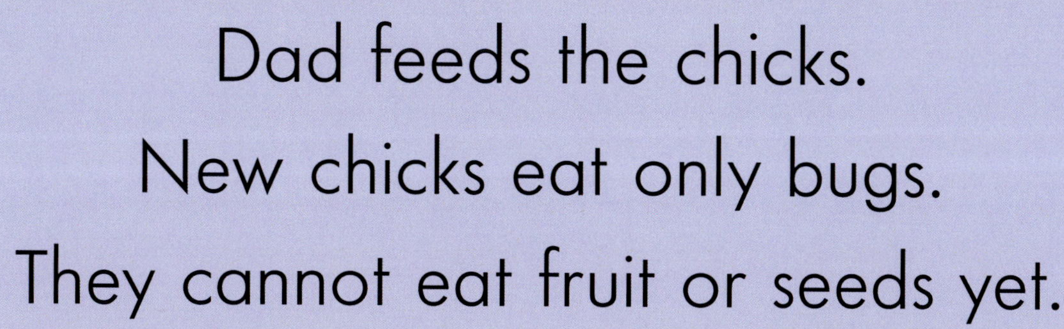

Dad feeds the chicks.
New chicks eat only bugs.
They cannot eat fruit or seeds yet.

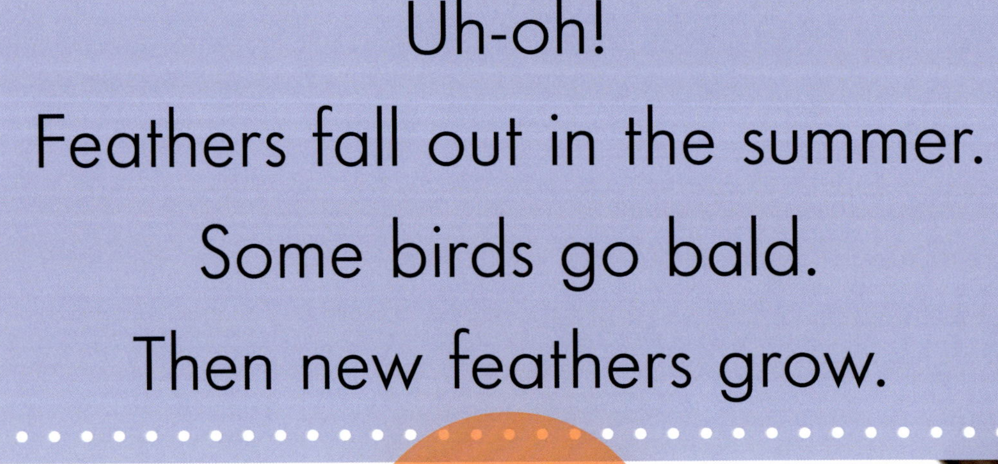

Uh-oh!
Feathers fall out in the summer.
Some birds go bald.
Then new feathers grow.

bald

The bird has a thick bill.
It can crack peanuts open.

A cardinal is a backyard bird.
Have you seen it?

crest

nest

Did you find?

bald

bill

Spot is published by Amicus Learning, an imprint of Amicus
P.O. Box 227, Mankato, MN 56002
www.amicuspublishing.us

Cataloging-in-Publication data is available
from the Library of Congress.
Library Binding ISBN: 9798892008303
Paperback ISBN: 9798892008969
eBook ISBN: 9798892009621

LCCN: 2025010590

Ana Brauer, editor
Deb Miner, series designer
Sara Hood, book designer
and photo researcher

Photos by Alamy Stock Photo/B Christopher, 2, 6–7, 15, Ivan Kuzmin, 8–9; Getty Images/Beata Whitehead, 2, 10–11, 15, Gary Carter, 2, 12–13, 15, MD. SHARIFUL ISLAM / 500px, 1, Rolf Nussbaumer, 2, 4–5, 15; Pixabay/Hans Toom, cover, 16, meganzopf, 3; Shutterstock/Bonnie Taylor Barry, 14